This book is dedicated to my wife Katherine,
who has spent decades forgiving me.

"You must change your hearts – for the kingdom of Heaven has arrived."

~~~*Jesus*

Compiled by Arthur Zeigler

Forgiving Your World

With Exercises in Forgiving the World

The Words of Jesus Concerning Forgiveness, Love, the Kingdom of Heaven and the Nature of God

Published by Desktop Prepress Services, http://www.desktopprepress.com

Cover images furnished by Jan Will © 2009 at http://www.istockphoto.com

ISBN: 978-0-578-04693-8

Printed in the United States of America

Foreword

This book is presented in two parts: The Words of Jesus and Forgiving Your World. The first part presents old material in a new way in order to clarify it. The second part explains a new concept in the application of forgiveness to our daily lives for the purpose of changing and improving our reality. Both parts are radical departures from the usual approaches.

The earliest copy of a New Testament gospel that has come down to us through the millennia is a copy of Saint Luke's Gospel, known as the Bodmer Papyrus XIV-XV. It belongs to the Vatican Library and can be dated from between AD 175-225. The document consists of fifty-one pages of a manuscript that is believed to originally have contained seventy-two pages.

A small fragment of papyrus, the Saint John Fragment, bearing portions of five verses of the Gospel of John is variously estimated to be about the same age.

We do not have any written record of the teachings of Jesus that date from less than 150 years after his death. We do not have any gospel written in Aramaic, the language that he probably spoke. We have no way of knowing how long the teachings of Jesus existed as an oral tradition passed down through generations before they were translated into Greek and put into writing. In addition to this, Biblical scholars believe the copies of the Gospels that have come down to us bear the marks of additions and improvements added by later authors.

After the First Council of Constantinople, called by the Roman Emperor Constantine in AD 381, the Roman Empire suppressed with all of its might those gospels that the newly established official religion did not authorize.

For all of these reasons, it has become difficult to know at this point in time—so far removed from the events of the life of Jesus—what parts of the Gospels handed down to us in the New Testament are his actual teaching and what authors have distorted beyond recognition and recovery.

Part One, The Words of Jesus, takes a fresh approach to these problems, and the author sincerely hopes the result will enable the reader to gain a clearer understanding of the unique and profound qualities of the teachings of Jesus. Part Two, Forgiving Your World, presents a new method, developed by the author, of thoroughly applying the forgiveness teachings of Jesus to all aspects of life, so the benefits of forgiveness can rapidly manifest.

It is no secret that negative emotions such as anger, envy, vindictiveness and hatred corrode the vessel that contains them. Often these emotions and the events that engendered them become repressed to the degree that they become part of the unconscious mind. That they are no longer part of the conscious mind does not mean that they cannot continue to adversely affect lives. Even if these negative emotions are festering below the surface of consciousness, they can be altering the ability to perceive reality correctly.

In recent years, the field of psychology has begun to recognize the importance of forgiveness, and a new school of psychology, known as Forgiveness Therapy, has come onto the scene as a major player. The well-known American psychiatrist Karl Menninger once said that if he could convince his psychiatric hospital patients that their sins were forgiven, three quarters of them could walk out the next day.

In addition to dealing with material in the conscious mind, the method presented in this book has the benefit of addressing material in the unconscious mind without going through the emotional upheaval of therapy and without having to reveal one's most private thoughts to a stranger. No therapist or intermediary of any kind is necessary other than the Holy Spirit, and it requires no complex system of analysis. The method is simple and powerful. It applies the two-thousand-year-old teachings of Jesus to the world of today in an easy and effective manner. It is the author's profound hope that the reader will find their reality illuminated with the daily use of the material and exercises provided in Part Two.

Contents

Part One: The Words of Jesus

Part Two: Forgiving Your World

Part One: The Words of Jesus

Chapter 1
What Did Jesus Say?

What did Jesus teach? What did he actually say? After 2,000 years, is it possible to know? The purpose of the First Council of Nicaea, called by the Roman Emperor Constantine in AD 325, was to establish a consensus, a uniformity, of teaching and belief for all the Christians of that time.

At this council and others that followed, the majority of bishops decided which of the many versions of the gospel then in existence to authorize as true and which of the various Christian beliefs would become the official version for the newly established, exclusive state religion of the Roman Empire. The council declared any teachings, beliefs and gospels not authorized by the majority as heresy and eradicated them with the full force and might of Roman Empire.

It was an exercise in mind control that lasted from AD 325 through the Spanish Inquisition. Under the direction of the Roman Empire and the Church of Rome, a great number of dissenting Christians died. The suppression and book burning were so thorough that some gospels disappeared from the face of the Earth for millennia, and we know of them only by references in letters and other writings that have survived.

In the Gospels of Matthew, Mark, Luke and John, do we have all of the teachings of Jesus or was a great deal lost? According to many biblical scholars, these Gospels were rewritten and extensively edited. Some propose that these improvements include the miracle stories and a virgin birth in order to support the claims that Jesus was a God. Even worse, it has been said that words were put in the mouth of Jesus by some of those writers and editors to support various factions of church politics with divine utterances.

So how does one know what was actually said by Jesus?

According to those who believe in the inerrancy of the Bible, it is totally without error and free from contradiction; however, according to most biblical scholars, only a lesser portion of the supposed words of Jesus can actually be attributed to him with any degree of certainty.

Understanding then, that Jesus did speak some of these words, we must ask: What did Jesus really say?

Thomas Jefferson endeavored to answer that question by extracting from the Gospels only the words attributed to Jesus and then looking for repetition of those words in more than one Gospel. He took those multiple quotations to reliably be the true sayings of Jesus. During the last century, modern biblical scholars have used much the same method for the same purpose.

While this might seem like a valid approach to confirm authenticity, there are two problems with it. First, it makes the assumption that unless a statement is made and then copied by others, it cannot be true. However, an author might not incorporate an unpopular statement into his own writing. It is also a possibility that the author did not know of the statement. In regards to this, such a single statement might be true, but it would not be accepted as valid. The second difficulty is that an error repeated by others is still an error. From the distance in time of two millennia, such a method is not reliable.

Is there, then, a method of extracting the true teachings of Jesus from the Gospels apart from expedient improvisations and improvements mixed together with dubious history? Can such a method also satisfy those who believe in inerrancy that truth is being brought to light and clarified? It may be that there is such a method.

If we ask ourselves what is unique about the Gospels, one thing shines forth that is practically without precedent in the Western World. It is not the virgin birth and claims of divinity. Those were common elements of a number of contemporary religions. Nor is it the ideas of blood sacrifice and a scapegoat to assume sins. These were part of the Jewish culture in which the story of Jesus took place.

Due to the recent occupation of their country by Romans, the Jews of the time of Jesus were under tremendous pressure culturally, linguistically, politically and religiously. Faction strove against faction and against their Roman overlords until the Romans exterminated a large portion of the Jewish population and drove much of the rest out of their homeland as punishment for resistance to Roman rule.

The story of Jesus seethes with this violence, and we are told that he narrowly escaped death by stoning for his heretical teachings—the teachings for which he ultimately was executed by crucifixion.

So in this time of ubiquitous hatred and violence, what was so different about the teachings of Jesus that set them apart from the cultural milieu in which they took place?

The easy answer to this question is the teaching of forgiveness and love as a way of life and a pathway to the kingdom of heaven, and the teaching that salvation is available without sacrifice simply by choosing it and rejecting hatred, anger and fear.

Prior to the time of Jesus, the teaching of universal forgiveness was not a widespread concept in Western civilization. In the East, in India, it was an aspect of the Hindu religion, but a minor aspect. In Buddhism, forgiveness was practiced to prevent disturbing one's mental well-being with unpleasantness. In the West, hatred and vengeance ruled the day. In the Middle-East, the Jews practiced forgiveness if one repented and pleaded for pardon, but forgiveness was considered to be conditional and discretionary for both man and God.

It was not until the teaching of Jesus that the idea of unconditional forgiveness became disseminated in the Western world. When we examine the Gospels with this unique teaching as our guide, extracting the reported words of Jesus regarding forgiveness and love, the apparent contradictions in the Gospels and the teachings of Jesus are left behind, and we obtain a clear and coherent message with relevance to us in the here and now. With this in mind, let us examine what Jesus said concerning love and forgiveness.

Chapter 2
The Words of Jesus Concerning Love and Forgiveness

"From that time Jesus began to preach and to say, '**You must change your hearts—for the kingdom of heaven has arrived.**'" Matthew 4:17

Luke 15:11-19: Jesus continued: "**There was a man who had two sons. The younger one said to his father, 'Father, give me my share of the estate.' So he divided his property between them.**

"**Not long after that, the younger son got together all he had, set off for a distant country and there squandered his wealth in wild living. After he had spent everything, there was a severe famine in that whole country, and he began to be in need. So he went and hired himself out to a citizen of that country, who sent him to his fields to feed pigs. He longed to fill his stomach with the pods that the pigs were eating, but no one gave him anything.**

"**When he came to his senses, he said, 'How many of my father's hired men have food to spare, and here I am starving to death! I will** set out and go back to my father and say to him: Father, I have sinned against heaven and against you. I am no longer worthy to be called your son; make me like one of your hired men.'

Luke 15:20-24: **"So he got up and went to his father. But while he was still a long way off, his father saw him and was filled with compassion for him; he ran to his son, threw his arms around him and kissed him.**

"The son said to him, 'Father, I have sinned against heaven and against you. I am no longer worthy to be called your son.'

"But the father said to his servants, 'Quick! Bring the best robe and put it on him. Put a ring on his finger and sandals on his feet. Bring the fattened calf and kill it. Let's have a feast and celebrate. For this son of mine was dead and is alive again; he was lost and is found.' So they began to celebrate.

Luke 15:25-32: **"Meanwhile, the older son was in the field. When he came near the house, he heard music and dancing. So he called one of the servants and asked him what was going on. 'Your brother has come,' he replied, 'and your father has killed the fattened calf because he has him back safe and sound.'**

"The older brother became angry and refused to go in. So his father went out and pleaded with him. But he answered his father, 'Look! All these years I've been slaving for you and never disobeyed your orders. Yet you never gave me even a young goat so I could celebrate with my friends. But when this son of yours who has squandered your property with prostitutes comes home, you kill the fattened calf for him!'

" 'My son,' the father said, 'you are always with me, and everything I have is yours. But we had to celebrate and be glad, because this brother of yours was dead and is alive again; he was lost and is found.' "

Part of the reason that Jesus taught in parables is because he was frequently accused of teaching heresy. The Parable of the Prodigal Son refutes the fable of Genesis. According to the teaching of Jesus, the son left the Kingdom of God by his own choosing without any influence from an anti-god or betrayal into original sin by his mate. By his own choice he left his father's home, wasting his inheritance and birthright; yet, he was not condemned by the father in any way. The son was able to return to his father's home, the Kingdom of God, without sacrifice or ritual and with no more action required than making the decision to return home.

The first choice made by the son was an error, and when he came to that awareness, all he needed to do was make a new choice. Then he was automatically restored to his father's love and his original home as if he had never left.

The religions of the time of Jesus required ritual and sacrifice. Many required a priestly intermediary between the penitent and the divine, but Jesus mentions none of these requirements in the Parable of the Prodigal Son. In this story, there is no sacrificial lamb to be slaughtered on an altar or a scapegoat to be driven into the wilderness. There is no need of another to intercede for the son. He is not judged by his father in any way. He is restored to the presence of his father and his father's home simply by returning home.

It's easy to see how such teaching would offend the priestly class of a culture that was given over to stringent dietary rules, ritual sexual mutilation, and blood sacrifice, and which promoted murder by mobs with stones. In fact, not only was stoning sanctioned, it was considered to be a righteous duty.

The truth that Jesus taught, then, was as revolutionary as it was heretical. Cloaking those teachings in parables was not enough to prevent him from ultimately being executed for heresy. There are other statements of Jesus that are relevant to the Parable of the Prodigal Son and support its teachings.

John 5:22: **"Moreover, the Father judges no one, but has entrusted all judgment to the Son."**

The son in the parable was his own judge and lived a life of self-condemnation until he chose to return to the father. He was in no way judged by the father as anything other than worthy of his father's love. Jesus taught that forgiveness does not require sacrifice.

Matthew 9:13: **"But go and learn what this means:'I desire mercy, not sacrifice.' For I have not come to call the righteous, but sinners."**

In the parable, the father requires no sacrifice from his son. The son may return to the presence of the father at any time and without precondition by simply doing so. He has only to set his foot on the path home to start the process. This principle was so important to Jesus that he said it again when his disciples were accused by the Pharisees of breaking the Sabbath law by gathering food.

Matthew 12:7-8: **"If you had known what these words mean,'I desire mercy, not sacrifice,' you would not have condemned the innocent. For the Son of Man is Lord of the Sabbath."**

The term Son of Man was used in both the Old and New Testaments to mean either a human being or ideal man. Again Jesus calls for mercy not sacrifice. As God is not judgmental and is all-merciful, Jesus instructed that we must be the same. The following verses are examples of his teachings that show these concepts.

Luke 6:36: **"Be merciful, just as your Father is merciful."**

Luke 6:37-38: **"Do not judge, and you will not be judged. Do not condemn, and you will not be condemned. Forgive, and you will be forgiven. Give, and it will be given to you. A good measure, pressed down, shaken together and running over, will be poured into your lap. For with the measure you use, it will be measured to you."**

Matthew 7:3-5 & Luke 6:41-42: **"Why do you look at the speck of sawdust in your brother's eye and pay no attention to the plank in your own eye? How can you say to your brother,'Let me take the speck** out of your eye,' when all the time there is a plank in your own eye? You hypocrite, first take the plank out of your own eye, and then you will see clearly to remove the speck from your brother's eye."

Luke 12:13-14: Someone in the crowd said to him, "Teacher, tell my brother to divide the inheritance with me."

Jesus replied, **"Man, who appointed me a judge or an arbiter between you?"**

John 8:15: **"You judge by human standards; I pass judgment on no one."**

John 12:47: **"As for the person who hears my words but does not keep them, I do not judge him. For I did not come to judge the world, but to save it."**

Aside from the Parable of the Prodigal Son, there is another story that also shows the nonjudgmental attitude of Jesus. The story of the woman caught in adultery is a model of mercy and forgiveness. There has been some controversy amongst biblical scholars on whether it should be included as an authentic part of the Gospel of John. How could it not be, since it exemplifies the teaching of Jesus concerning forgiveness?

John 8:2-5: At dawn he appeared again in the temple courts, where all the people gathered around him, and he sat down to teach them. The teachers of the law and the Pharisees brought in a woman caught in adultery. They made her stand before the group and said to Jesus, "Teacher, this woman was caught in the act of adultery. In the Law Moses commanded us to stone such women. Now what do you say?"

John 8:6-11: They were using this question as a trap, in order to have a basis for accusing him.

But Jesus bent down and started to write on the ground with his finger. When they kept on questioning him, he straightened up and said to them, **"If any**

one of you is without sin, let him be the first to throw a stone at her." Again he stooped down and wrote on the ground.

At this, those who heard began to go away one at a time, the older ones first, until only Jesus was left, with the woman still standing there. Jesus straightened up and asked her, **"Woman, where are they? Has no one condemned you?"**

"No one, sir," she said.

"Then neither do I condemn you," Jesus declared. **"Go now and leave your life of sin."**

There are other scriptures where Jesus mentions a judgmental attitude. One can be found in Matthew 7:1 & 2: **"Don't criticize people, and you will not be criticized. For you will be judged by the way you criticize others, and the measure you give will be the measure you receive."**

Jesus instructed that learning to forgive others is essential to our own salvation. This is a very important principle and it is counterintuitive. Because of this, it should be studied thoroughly and practiced until it becomes an automatic part of our lives. We must learn to forgive the sins of others so that our own sins can be forgiven. Even self-forgiveness can not take place until we learn to forgive others, because we see our own flaws mirrored outside ourselves (and that is where forgiveness must start).

Matthew 6:14: **"For if you forgive other people their failures, your Heavenly Father will also forgive you."**

Matthew 7:12: **"Treat other people exactly as you would like to be treated by them—this is the essence of all true religion."**

Luke 6:31: **"Treat men exactly as you would like them to treat you."**

Mark 11:25-26: **"And when you stand praying, if you hold anything against anyone, forgive him, so that your Father in heaven may forgive you your sins."**

An important lesson in forgiveness is told in both Matthew and Luke—the story of Jesus healing the paralytic.

Luke 5:17-20: One day as he was teaching, Pharisees and teachers of the law, who had come from every village of Galilee and from Judea and Jerusalem, were sitting there. And the power of the Lord was present for him to heal the sick. Some men came carrying a paralytic on a mat and tried to take him into the house to lay him before Jesus. When they could not find a way to do this because of the crowd, they went up on the roof and lowered him on his mat through the tiles into the middle of the crowd, right in front of Jesus. When Jesus saw their faith, he said, **"Friend, your sins are forgiven."**

Matthew 9:3-8: "At this, some of the teachers of the law said to themselves, "This fellow is blaspheming!"

Knowing their thoughts, Jesus said, **"Why do you entertain evil thoughts in your hearts? Which is easier: to say, 'Your sins are forgiven,' or to say, 'Get up and walk'? But so that you may know that the Son of Man has authority on earth to forgive sins...."** Then he said to the paralytic, **"Get up, take your mat and go home."** And the man got up and went home. When the crowd saw this, they were filled with awe; and they praised God, who had given such authority to men.

In this story, we are taught that men have the power and the ability to forgive sin and that such forgiveness can be a means of healing. How much and to what extent we should forgive others is told in Matthew.

Matthew 18:21: Then Peter came to Jesus and asked, "Lord, how many times shall I forgive my brother when he sins against me? Up to seven times?"

Matthew 18:22: Jesus answered, **"I tell you, not seven times, but seventy-seven times."**

One of the important teachings of Jesus is that we must love our fellow man, but this is impossible until we have forgiven him. Only after we have incorporated the teaching of forgiveness into our lives on a daily basis, can we begin to appreciate our humanity and truly love our neighbor and our creator. It is so important, that we must make it a constant part of our reality.

The following verses all illustrate and instruct how we can learn to forgive the sins of others and learn to love our neighbors. It is by doing this that we can learn to forgive our own sins and learn to love ourselves. Then we can begin to see ourselves as God sees us all—worthy of love.

Matthew 9:10-13: While Jesus was having dinner at Matthew's house, many tax collectors and "sinners" came and ate with him and his disciples. When the Pharisees saw this, they asked his disciples, "Why does your teacher eat with tax collectors and 'sinners'?"

On hearing this, Jesus said, **"It is not the healthy who need a doctor, but the sick. But go and learn what this means: 'I desire mercy, not sacrifice.' For I have not come to call the righteous, but sinners."**

Luke 6:32-35: **"If you love those who love you, what credit is that to you? Even 'sinners' love those who love them. And if you do good to those who are good to you, what credit is that to you? Even 'sinners' do that. And if you lend to those from whom you expect repayment, what credit is that to you? Even 'sinners' lend to 'sinners,' expecting to be repaid in full. But love your enemies, do good to them, and lend to them without expecting to get anything back. Then your reward will be great, and you will be sons of the Most High, because he is kind to the ungrateful and wicked.**

Matthew 5:43-45: **"You have heard that it was said, 'Love your neighbor and hate your enemy.' But I tell you: Love your enemies and pray for those who persecute you, that you may be sons of your**

Father in heaven. He causes his sun to rise on the evil and the good, and sends rain on the righteous and the unrighteous."

Matthew 5:46-48: **"If you love those who love you, what reward will you get? Are not even the tax collectors doing that? And if you greet only your brothers, what are you doing more than others? Do not even pagans do that? Be perfect, therefore, as your heavenly Father is perfect."**

Luke 6:27-28: **"But I tell you who hear me: Love your enemies, do good to those who hate you, bless those who curse you, pray for those who mistreat you."**

Luke 6:29a: **"If someone strikes you on one cheek, turn to him the other also."**

Luke 6:29b-30: **"If someone takes your cloak, do not stop him from taking your tunic. Give to everyone who asks you, and if anyone takes what belongs to you, do not demand it back."**

Mark 12:28: One of the teachers of the law came and heard them debating. Noticing that Jesus had given them a good answer, he asked him, "Of all the commandments, which is the most important?"

Mark 12:29-31: **"The most important one,"** answered Jesus, **"is this: 'Hear, O Israel, the Lord our God, the Lord is one. Love the Lord your God with all your heart and with all your soul and with all your mind and with all your strength.' The second is this: 'Love your neighbor as yourself.' There is no commandment greater than these."**

Mark 12:32-33: "Well said, teacher," the man replied. "You are right in saying that God is one and there is no other but him. To love him with all your heart, with all your understanding and with all your strength, and to love your neighbor as yourself is more important than all burnt offerings and sacrifices."

Mark 12:34: Then Jesus, noting the thoughtfulness of his reply, said to him, **"You are not far from the kingdom of God!"** After this nobody felt like asking him any more questions.

In the Gospel of John, Jesus told his disciples that they must love one an-other.

John 15:9: **"I have loved you just as the Father has loved me. You must go on living in my love."**

John 13:34: **"A new command I give you: Love one another. As I have loved you, so you must love one another."**

When instructing his followers how to pray, Jesus again mentions that even in conversation with God, we should tell that we have forgiven those against whom we might otherwise hold a grievance.

Luke 11:2-4: He said to them, **"When you pray, say: Father, hallowed be your name, your kingdom come. Give us each day our daily bread. Forgive us our sins, for we also forgive everyone who sins against us. And lead us not into temptation."**

The benefits of prayer are described by Jesus in Matthew.

Matthew 7:7-8: **"Ask and it will be given to you; seek and you will find; knock and the door will be opened to you. For everyone who asks receives; he who seeks finds; and to him who knocks, the door will be opened."**

Matthew 7:9-11: **"Which of you, if his son asks for bread, will give him a stone? Or if he asks for a fish, will give him a snake? If you, then, though you are evil, know how to give good gifts to your children, how much more will your Father in heaven give good gifts to those who ask him."**

According to the Gospel of Luke, Jesus practiced forgiveness even during the anguish of his crucifixion.

Luke 23:32-34: Two other men, both criminals, were also led out with him to be executed. When they came to the place called the Skull, there they cruci-fied him, along with the criminals—one on his right, the other on his left. Jesus said, **"Father, forgive them, for they do not know what they are doing."** And they divided up his clothes by casting lots.

The Gospel of John reports that after the crucifixion Jesus told his disciples they must forgive sins. He also made clear the consequences if they failed to do so.

John 20:23: **"If you forgive anyone his sins, they are forgiven; if you do not forgive them, they are not forgiven."**

Certainly we can not love those who remain unforgiven. First, we must for-give, and then we can learn to love. It is our task to make sure that none re-main unforgiven by us, and it is a job that can be done only by us.

Chapter 3
The Words of Jesus Concerning the Kingdom of Heaven

"I tell you the truth, some who are standing here will not taste death before they see the kingdom of God come with power." ~ Jesus

From the teaching of Jesus about forgiveness, we have learned that we must be merciful, forgiving and nonjudgmental so that we can love our fellow man and our creator. When forgiveness becomes a way of life, it becomes possible for the Kingdom of God to manifest in our reality. According to the words of Jesus, it needs only the smallest entry point.

Matthew 5:2-9: Then he began his teaching by saying to them, **"How happy are the humble-minded, for the kingdom of Heaven is theirs! How happy are those who know what sorrow means for they will be given courage and comfort! Happy are those who claim nothing, for the whole earth will belong to them! Happy are those who are hungry and thirsty for goodness, for they will be fully satisfied! Happy are the merciful, for they will have mercy shown to them! Happy are the utterly sincere, for they will see God! Happy are**

those who make peace, for they will be sons of God!"

Luke 13:20-21: Again he asked, **"What shall I compare the kingdom of God to? It is like yeast that a woman took and mixed into a large amount of flour until it worked all through the dough."**

It takes a very small amount of yeast mixed in with a large amount of flour to have an impressive effect.

Luke 13:18-19: Then Jesus asked, **"What is the kingdom of God like? What shall I compare it to? It is like a mustard seed, which a man took and planted in his garden. It grew and became a tree, and the birds of the air perched in its branches."**

Mark 9:1: And he said to them, **"I tell you the truth, some who are standing here will not taste death before they see the kingdom of God come with power."**

Mark 12:13-15a: Later they sent some of the Pharisees and Herodians to Jesus to catch him in his words. They came to him and said, "Teacher, we know you are a man of integrity. You aren't swayed by men, because you pay no attention to who they are; but you teach the way of God in accordance with the truth. Is it right to pay taxes to Caesar or not? Should we pay or shouldn't we?"

Mark 12:15b: But Jesus saw through their hypocrisy and said to them, **"Why try this trick on me? Bring me a coin and let me look at it."**

Mark 12:16: They brought the coin, and he asked them, **"Whose portrait is this? And whose inscription?"**

"Caesar's," they replied.

Mark 12:17: Then Jesus said to them, **"Give to Caesar what is Caesar's and to God what is God's."** And they were amazed at him.

Scripture makes a very plain statement that the Kingdom of Heaven is not a kingdom of this world. It is further clarified in the following verses.

Luke 17:20-21: Once, having been asked by the Pharisees when the kingdom of God would come, Jesus replied, **"The kingdom of God does not come with your careful observation, nor will people say, 'Here it is,' or 'There it is,' because the kingdom of God is within you."**

John 3:3: In reply Jesus declared, **"I tell you the truth, no one can see the kingdom of God unless he is born again."**

John 3:6-7: **"Flesh gives birth to flesh, but the Spirit gives birth to spirit. You should not be surprised at my saying, 'You must be born again."**

These teachings make clear that the kingdom of God is not of this world, but with only the smallest of opportunities which forgiveness allows, it can manifest in us and through us as spirit gives birth to spirit and we are spiritually "born again."

Part Two: Forgiving Your World

Chapter 4
The World of Illusion and the Forgiveness of Things

Much, perhaps all, that we see and experience in this world is illusion, at least to the extent that we are blinded by our preconceptions. Acting as blinders against reality are all of our earlier judgments about things that we have made. In some cases, others have made the judgments, and we have agreed with them. Judgments, such as political beliefs and religious dogma, eliminate whole categories of things from true examination because of preconceptions.

Our perception of reality and the things associated with it is altered by the degree that we dislike, despise or fear something or consider it inferior to another thing. If we do not remove these negative aspects, our reality will be filtered through them. Life in this world necessitates making judgments in order to survive: satiety as opposed to hunger, comfort as opposed to pain, safety as opposed to danger, love as opposed to hate and good as opposed to evil. In this way, two valued logic systems arise, and false perceptions rule our reality as we see all things in terms of black and white.

Between what we arbitrarily think of as darkness and light are many degrees of partial light, so darkness is in fact the absence of light to one degree or another and not in most cases an absolute. What we see as evil by our judgmental standards is only an absence of goodness, an arbitrary and subjective perception and not a thing in and of itself.

The name of a thing is but a symbol for it and not the thing itself. To each name, each symbol, we attach a set of connotations. When we manipulate those symbols in thinking or in speaking, we alter our perception of the thing named, twisting away from actuality because of the two valued logic sets attached to the symbols that we give to things.

We imbibe these judgments with our mother's milk as infants, when we learn language. It is natural for people to enter the vale of illusion without realizing they have done so. The experiences of our lives from infancy to death are a lie to the degree that we leave those judgments unexamined and to the degree that things are consciously, or more probably unconsciously, unforgiven.

I have found a way to gain mental clarity, happiness and peace by forgiving the names of things. I call this forgiving the things of the world. As we go through life we often curse the thorn that pierces our flesh or the stone that bruises our foot. After we hit our thumb with a hammer, we have a conscious, or more probably unconscious, association of fear and pain with hammers. We attach similar associations to many of the things that surround us, and to that extent, we become the victims of our own flinching away from the world.

The name for a thing is a symbol for that item. As we gain experience in life, these symbols become so freighted with meaning that it is the symbol we perceive instead of the thing itself. We hold these illusions in place unless we forgive the things of this world as well as our fellow man.

Jesus taught that we must forgive our brothers and sisters, and by extension, we can learn to forgive the entire physical universe in which we find ourselves.

The exercises in the following chapter are offered in the hope that you may extend forgiveness in your life and thereby increase awareness of your nature as a spiritual being. They are a methodical means of rapidly extending the benefits of forgiveness into all areas of your reality. Proceed to do the exercises with complete confidence, because the only way that you can fail to have a good outcome is if you don't do the work.

Have fun with it, because forgiveness is not a grim task. As you proceed, you will find it to be a delight that will brighten your existence.

It is an opportunity to lay down your burdens of anger, hatred, fear and memories of pain and painful situations. It can be a great relief and occasion for joy.

If for any reason you get bogged down in the practice of these exercises, just put them aside for a few days and then return to them later. There is no hurry to race through the lists, because every day can use some forgiveness. Plus, it is important to establish, over time, a habit of daily forgiveness until it becomes second nature.

After all, what else could you possibly do that would be more important than helping to bring the Kingdom of Heaven to this troubled reality in which we find ourselves? How else can you increase your awareness that all of God's children, including yourself, are loved by God and are worthy of love?

Chapter 5
Exercises in Forgiveness

"If the doors of perception were cleansed
everything would appear to man as it is: Infinite." ~ William Blake

Defining Terms:
The symbols that we use to identify things are the names that we give them. As a part of speech these are know as nouns. The word noun comes from the Latin *nomen* meaning "name." Nouns are those expressions that refer to a person, place, thing, event, substance, quality or idea.

The Method:
Jesus taught the necessity of forgiving people, and we will do so as part of these exercises. We will also forgive places, things, events, substances, qualities and ideas. Since we are by definition not consciously aware of the content of our unconscious minds, we will learn to forgive everything that we can call to mind about a certain subject and give what we can not recall over to the Holy Spirit to deal with in the manner most beneficial to the manifestation of the kingdom of heaven into our reality.

What to Forgive:
In the next chapter, lists of nouns that are candidates for forgiveness will be presented. There are lists of persons, places, things, events, substances, qualities,

emotions and ideas. All that is necessary to do is to proceed through the lists, taking each item in its turn and inserting it into the forgiveness formula. If you wish to forgive items not on the lists, do not hesitate to do so. There is no shortage of things to forgive as our aim is to forgive the entire world and everything in it incrementally.

Step One—Find It:

The first phrase in the forgiveness formula is:
Call to mind a _____ *that is not forgiven.*

For an example, we will insert the first item from the first list of nouns. The phrase then becomes: Call to mind a <u>father</u> who is not forgiven.

To do the exercise in forgiveness, find a quiet place, assume a restful position, close your eyes and repeat the first phrase, for example: Call to mind a <u>father</u> who is not forgiven. Then look into your mind as if you are remembering. It is not necessary to actually remember, because you will find something there to forgive whether it is a memory or something else. It may be a picture of a memory or it may be an area of density, darkness, sensation or emotion in the mind. Once you have settled on a thing in some part of your mind, no matter what it is that has responded to the first phrase, use the next phrase in the formula.

Step Two—Forgive It:

The second phrase in the forgiveness formula is:
I forgive _____ *and everything associated with it. It doesn't matter anymore. I forgive it completely.*

To continue with the example that we used before, the second phrase would be: I forgive <u>father</u> and everything associated with him. It doesn't matter anymore. I forgive him completely.

Step Three—Give the Forgiveness to the Holy Spirit:

The third phrase in the formula is: *I give my forgiveness to the Holy Spirit to complete and to use in the way most beneficial for the manifestation of the kingdom of God in my reality.*

An event of forgiveness is a worthy gift for the Holy Spirit, and in return you can expect the Holy Spirit to aid you in your endeavor.

The Procedure:

When you use this three-step formula you can expect to feel relief, happiness, joy, elation and even ecstasy. If you don't feel this the first time with any given item from the lists as you go through the forgiveness formula, go through it again as follows: *Call to mind another* _____ *that is not forgiven.*

To continue with the example that we used before, the phrase would be: Call to mind another <u>father</u> that is not forgiven.

Again, as before, when you look into your mind you will find something that responds to the inquiry. What ever you find, that is what you will forgive. The rest of the formula would remain the same.

If after going through the forgiveness formula the second time for a particular item from the lists, you do not feel relief, happiness, joy, elation or ecstasy then proceed to a second variation of phrase number one of the formula as follows: *Call to mind a* _____ *that another has not forgiven.*

To continue with the example that we used before, the phrase would be: Call to mind a <u>father</u> that another has not forgiven. This means call to mind a <u>father</u> that another person has not forgiven.

Again, as before, when you look into your mind you will find something that responds to the inquiry. What ever you find, that is what you will forgive. The rest of the formula would remain the same.

These three versions of the forgiveness formula are extremely powerful, and you can expect them to transform your reality. When you use them for even a short time, perhaps only a few minutes, you will realize that something un-precedented has taken place. When you get a feeling of great relief, happiness, joy, elation or ecstasy, then it is time to take a break from the work until nor-malcy has returned. Don't worry about how long it takes to work your way through the lists, because it does not matter. You are changing your reality for the better every time that you do the work of forgiveness, and if you run out of things to forgive, then go through the lists again or make your own.

For the sake of clarity the three versions of the forgiveness formula are presented next.

Version One:

Call to mind a _____ that is not forgiven.

I forgive _____ and everything associated with it. It doesn't matter anymore. I forgive it completely.

I give my forgiveness to the Holy Spirit to complete and to use in the way most beneficial for the manifestation of the kingdom of God in my reality.

Version Two:

Call to mind another _____ that is not forgiven.

I forgive _____ and everything associated with it. It doesn't matter anymore. I forgive it completely.

I give my forgiveness to the Holy Spirit to complete and to use in the way most beneficial for the manifestation of the kingdom of God in my reality.

Version Three:

Call to mind a _____ that another has not forgiven.

I forgive _____ and everything associated with it. It doesn't matter anymore. I forgive it completely.

I give my forgiveness to the Holy Spirit to complete and to use in the way most beneficial for the manifestation of the kingdom of God in my reality.

Chapter 6
Lists for Forgiveness

"What shall I compare the kingdom of God to? It is like yeast that a woman took and mixed into a large amount of flour until it worked all through the dough."~ Jesus

These lists are arbitrary collections and are not to be considered complete in any way. They are presented as an aid to help get you started on the work of forgiveness. You will find that they are, nevertheless, very effective when used as directed with the forgiveness formulas.

Ask the Holy Spirit to aid you in your work and give your forgiveness to the Holy Spirit in thanksgiving. It is a fitting and worthy gift. Working together with the Holy Spirit and each other, we can forgive the world and change our reality. Given the smallest of openings by us, the Holy Spirit enters into our reality and starts its healing work.

List of Persons

Father
Mother
Brother
Sister
Uncle
Aunt
Friend
Husband
Wife
Child
Lover
Teacher
Priest
Preacher
Boss
Employee
Co-worker
Administrator
Dentist
Doctor
Neighbor
Nurse
Policeman
Politician
Government worker
Jesus
Driver
Official
Soldier
Sailor
Singer
Musician
God
Author
Actor
President
Celebrity
Bum
Stranger
Self

List of Places

Home	Below
Living room	Freeway
Kitchen	Jail
Bathroom	Field
Bedroom	Church
Basement	River
Stairway	Stream
Attic	Lake
Crawlspace	Ocean
Sidewalk	Beach
Alley	Hospital
Hometown	Airport
Village	Woods
City	Forest
Countryside	Cemetery
State	Desert
Rest home	Mountain
Country	View
Above	Inside
Road	Outside

List of Things

Glass	Cat
Dish	Penis
Book	Vagina
Bible	Vegetable
Knife	Weed
Gun	Fruit
Bed	Animal
Toilet	Hand
Fork	Stain
Shoes	Paper
Underwear	Finger
Automobile	Toe
Airplane	Leg
Boat	Arm
Hammer	Head
Tool	Tooth
Machine	Stomach
Dog	Back
Clothing	Other body part
Face	Body

List of Events

Dance	Remembrance
Wedding	Returning
Vacation	Pregnancy
Service	Birth
Fight	Fall
Illness	Accident
Flight	Piercing
Divorce	Fire
Funeral	Injury
Election	Surgery
War	Death
Harvest	Journey
Hunger	Arrival
Graduation	Explosion
Meal	Storm
Date	Impact
Abandonment	Disaster
Sex	Treatment
Awakening	Dream
Forgetting	Separation

List of Substances

Water	Wood
Ice	Hair
Blood	Cloth
Glass	Rubber
Stone	Plastic
Feces	Paint
Oil	Clay
Cement	Flesh
Grease	Medicine
Snot	Drug
Urine	Leather
Bone	Fur
Ivory	Soap
Dust	Salt
Beer	Slime
Air	Fat
Wine	Gasoline
Metal	Alcohol
Dirt	Dandruff
Food	Vomit

List of Emotions

Sadness
Joy
Disgust
Acceptance
Anger
Fear
Anticipation
Surprise
Grief
Disappointment
Remorse
Contempt
Affection
Lust
Cheerfulness
Longing
Relief
Contentment
Shame
Apathy

Rage
Sympathy
Love
Horror
Envy
Hopelessness
Regret
Apprehension
Frustration
Loneliness
Humiliation
Boredom
Confusion
Pride
Disrespect
Hatred
Pleasure
Insecurity
Apprehension
Panic

List of Qualities

Smallness	Drunkenness
Saltiness	Rottenness
Coldness	Homelessness
Stickiness	Aloneness
Slickness	Fullness
Swollenness	Moistness
Putridness	Hopelessness
Denseness	Viciousness
Wetness	Stupidness
Flatness	Sadness
Filthiness	Restlessness
Hotness	Forgetfulness
Vastness	Scariness
Quickness	Moistness
Shyness	Sharpness
Meanness	Falseness
Slowness	Bluntness
Darkness	Deceitfulness
Distortion	Emptiness
Stench	Scarcity

List of Ideas

An idea of...

Impurity

Holiness

Filthiness

Unworthiness

Failure

Poverty

Waste

Depravity

Deception

Eternity

Being Lost

Impossibility

Separation

Being Alone

Hopelessness

Superiority

Inferiority

Duty

Being Late

Abandonment

Weakness

Scarcity

Death

Sadness

Danger

Jesus

God

Darkness

Light

Pain

Being found out

Returning

Remembering

Size

Bodies

Location

Being alone

Salvation

Eternity

Time

Chapter 7
Blessing Your World

"Bless those who curse you and pray for those who mistreat you."
--- Luke 6:28

The cleansing benefits of the forgiveness that you are exercising can be extended by pronouncing a blessing on those persons, places, things, events, substances, qualities or ideas that you have just forgiven.

This is very easy to do and the effect is great in proportion to the effort expended. This is so powerful and important that it is being presented to you as a separate item rather than including it with the Forgiveness Formula.

In each case after forgiving an item and giving the forgiveness to the Holy Spirit, assume a benevolent attitude toward the item and wish it well. This helps to remove any feelings of malice that you have been maintaining towards the item.

A form to use could be as follows:
I bless _____ and desire that <u>they, he, she or it</u> may know the joy of the kingdom of God.

The blessing that you give may or may not benefit the object of the blessing but it will most certainly alter your attitude towards it.

I have found that when I pull weeds in my garden and bless them as I do so, the experience is transformed and transformative.

The blessing does not alter the intent to get the weeding done or the consequences for the weeds but it does remove any hint of malice from the operation and that in turn alters attitude giving a clean and clear perspective.

Afterword

"What is the kingdom of God like? What shall I compare it to? It is like a mustard seed, which a man took and planted in his garden. It grew and became a tree, and the birds of the air perched in its branches." ~ Jesus

Forgiveness heals the forgiver as well as the forgiven, and it is the key that can unshackle us from the past. In many ways forgiveness is counter-intuitive. It is normal to feel anger, fear, hurt, resentment and rage when we have been harmed or treated cruelly by others.

Our survival instincts tell us that it is necessary to defend ourselves against harm, but if we spend a lifetime unconsciously defending ourselves against something that occurred long ago in our past, then we live a warped and fearful existence. By doing the work of going through the lists and forgiving persons, places, things, events, substances, qualities and ideas, we can eventually completely forgive the whole physical universe of time, space, energy and matter together with everyone and every thing in it.

What a wonderful idea. It certainly beats playing marbles or whatever other games you have been playing in your life. Sometimes it seems that complete universal forgiveness is unrealistic and not practical. After all, the number one rule in life is to survive, and it is easy to think that anyone and anything that impedes our survival is evil and should be suppressed or destroyed.

Does all this forgiving mean that we must force ourselves to associate with people who harm us or that we don't like? No of course not. It only means that we must forgive them completely so that we can get on with our lives, and we must forgive them **"seventy times seven"** if necessary.

Does forgiveness mean that we should not defend ourselves? I for one would do whatever was necessary to defend my family effectively. Most of us would not hesitate to restrain, or if necessary do violence to, someone viciously attacking a small child. Most us would also leap to the defense of our nation, if it was being attacked by an outside force, because survival is a basic instinct whether it is the survival of self, family or community.

Although forgiveness and blessing are always appropriate, extirpation is sometimes necessary.

For most of us, for the time being, forgiveness must take place after the fact of the event. Perhaps one day, in a more perfect world, we can aspire to practice what Jesus taught in the Gospel of Matthew.

Matthew 5:38-39: **"You have heard that it was said, 'Eye for eye, and tooth for tooth.' But I tell you, Do not resist an evil person. If some-one strikes you on the right cheek, turn to him the other also"**

Matthew5:40-42: **"And if someone wants to sue you and take your tunic, let him have your cloak as well. If someone forces you to go one mile, go with him two miles. Give to the one who asks you, and do not turn away from the one who wants to borrow from you."**

Matthew 5:43-45: **"You have heard that it was said, 'Love your neigh-bor and hate your enemy.' But I tell you: Love your enemies and pray for those who persecute you, that you may be sons of your Father in heaven. He causes his sun to rise on the evil and the good, and sends rain on the righteous and the unrighteous."**

Matthew 5:46-48: **"If you love those who love you, what reward will you get? Are not even the tax collectors doing that? And if you greet only your brothers, what are you doing more than others?**

Do not even pagans do that? Be perfect, therefore, as your heavenly Father is perfect."

As we practice forgiveness in our lives, we may in time gain the ability to apply even more of the radical teachings of Jesus to our lives. One of the good things about time is that we don't have to do everything at once. We can work at things incrementally.

The best quality of time is that it prevents us from making decisions which are eternal. Like the Prodigal Son, at any point in time, we can make another choice different from the one that is currently causing our ruin. We can choose to return to the kingdom of Heaven by making forgiveness a part of our lives.

The reason that forgiveness seems so counterintuitive is that it is an attribute of God. It is not of this world. The word holy implies otherness. Forgiveness is holy as it is a thing that is other than this world. Jesus knew and taught that forgiveness is of the kingdom of God and that being nonjudgmental is an attribute of God.

As we add the holiness of forgiveness to our lives, we give an entry point for the otherness of the kingdom of God to establish itself in our reality.

Luke 13:20-21: **Again he asked, "What shall I compare the kingdom of God to? It is like yeast that a woman took and mixed into a large amount of flour until it worked all through the dough."**

Index of Gospel Verses

The author has used two different translations to quote from in order to make the text easier to read and understand.

As beautiful as the archaic English language used in the King James version of the Bible is, it can be the cause of confusion to the modern reader.

For this reason whenever a verse of scripture in one text was clearer or the syntax was more friendly to the modern ear then the corresponding verse in the other text, the more reader friendly text was the one chosen to quote from.

The older forms of English from the many very good older translations of the New Testament can sound stilted to the modern reader and for this reason the two translations quoted in this book are two of the more recent works of scholarship.

On the following pages separate indexes are given for the verses quoted from each of those sources.

INDEX of GOSPEL VERSES

From the New International Version of the New Testament

INDEX of GOSPEL VERSES

From the JB Phillips Translation of the New Testament

Acknowledgements

The author is beholden to all of those spiritual teachers and writers who have, over the years, influenced his thinking and perception of reality.

A Prayer

Father, thank you for all the gifts that you have given me, especially those gifts that I am not yet aware of.

I pray that I may learn to surrender my will so that there is room for your grace to manifest in my life.

Help me to choose those alternatives that align with your inevitable will.

I pray that I may be more aware of and constantly conscious of the presence of your love.

Help me to allow myself to be filled with your love until it overflows and inundates my world.